ARTIFICIAL INTELLIGENCE AND GPT

Evolving Frontiers in the Next Era

Geoffrey Zachary

CONTENTS

Artificial Intelligence and GPT: Evolving Frontiers in the Next Era

Introduction:
Artificial Intelligence (AI) has become an integral part of our lives, revolutionizing the way we work, communicate, and interact with technology. From voice assistants and recommendation systems to autonomous vehicles and medical diagnosis, AI has permeated various sectors, bringing unprecedented advancements and possibilities.

One of the remarkable developments in AI is the emergence of Generative Pre-trained Transformers (GPT). GPT is a deep learning model that has garnered significant attention and praise for its ability to generate human-like text, understand context, and perform a wide range of natural language processing tasks.

The evolution of AI has been marked by a shift from rule-based systems to more sophisticated machine learning algorithms. Traditional AI approaches relied on explicit rules and predefined logic to solve specific problems. However, with the advent of deep learning, AI models like GPT can learn and generalize from large amounts of data, allowing them to tackle complex tasks and exhibit human-level performance in certain domains.

GPT leverages the power of neural networks and transformers, which are specialized architectures designed to process sequential data. By pre-training on vast amounts of text data, GPT learns to recognize patterns, understand language semantics, and generate coherent and contextually relevant responses.

The rise of GPT has opened new frontiers in natural language processing, enabling applications such as text generation, translation, summarization, and sentiment analysis. Its ability to understand context and generate human-like text has sparked both excitement and concerns about the potential impact of AI on various aspects of society.

In this book, we embark on a journey to explore the evolution and potential of GPT in the coming years. We will delve into its underlying principles, the technological advancements that have led to its development, and the challenges and opportunities it presents.

Throughout the book, we will examine real-life examples and case studies that highlight the transformative power of GPT. We will discuss its applications in industries such as healthcare, finance, marketing, and customer service, showcasing how GPT is reshaping workflows, enhancing productivity, and enabling innovative solutions.

Furthermore, we will address the ethical implications and considerations surrounding the use of GPT. As AI systems become more advanced and capable, questions arise regarding privacy, bias, accountability, and the potential displacement of human labour. We will explore these topics and provide insights into responsible AI development and deployment.

By gaining a comprehensive understanding of GPT and its evolution, we can better prepare ourselves for the future of AI and leverage its potential to drive positive change. Join us on this journey as we navigate the exciting world of artificial intelligence and explore the promising trajectory of Generative Pre-trained Transformers.

PART I: FOUNDATIONS OF ARTIFICIAL INTELLIGENCE

CHAPTER 1: HISTORY OF ARTIFICIAL INTELLIGENCE

Introduction:

Artificial Intelligence (AI) is a field of study and technology that aims to create intelligent machines capable of mimicking human cognitive functions. The history of AI spans several decades and is marked by significant advancements, setbacks, and breakthroughs. In this chapter, we will explore the key milestones and developments that have shaped the evolution of AI.

Early Beginnings:

The origins of AI can be traced back to the 1950s when researchers began exploring the idea of creating machines that could exhibit intelligent behaviour. The seminal work of Alan Turing and his concept of the "Turing Test" laid the foundation for evaluating machine intelligence. In 1956, the Dartmouth Conference marked the birth of AI as a formal research discipline, bringing together leading scientists to discuss the possibilities of creating artificial intelligence.

The AI Winter:

In the 1970s and 1980s, AI experienced a period known as the "AI Winter" characterized by waning interest and funding due to unmet expectations and limited progress. The high expectations set by early AI pioneers were not met, and the field faced significant challenges in developing intelligent systems that could handle real-world complexity. Funding for AI research dwindled, and the field entered a period of reduced activity.

Expert Systems and Knowledge-Based AI:

During the AI Winter, researchers shifted their focus to developing expert systems and knowledge-based AI. Expert systems used rule-based logic to mimic human expertise in specific domains. Examples include MYCIN, a system for diagnosing bacterial infections, and DENDRAL, a system for analysing chemical compounds. These systems demonstrated the potential of AI in solving specialized problems but had limitations in handling uncertainty and real-world complexity.

The Renaissance of AI:

In the 1990s, AI experienced a resurgence, fuelled by advancements in computing power, algorithmic innovations, and the availability of large-scale data. Machine learning, a subfield of AI, gained prominence with the development of algorithms that allowed machines to learn patterns and make predictions from data. Neural networks, inspired by the structure of the human brain, emerged as powerful tools for learning and pattern recognition.

The Era of Big Data and Deep Learning:

The 2000s witnessed a transformative shift in AI with the proliferation of big data and the rise of deep learning. The exponential growth of data, coupled with advancements in computational capabilities, enabled the training of deep neural networks on massive datasets. Deep learning models, such as convolutional neural networks (CNNs) and recurrent neural networks (RNNs), revolutionized fields like computer vision, natural language processing, and speech recognition.

Real-Life Examples:

Real-life examples demonstrate the practical applications and impact of AI throughout history. IBM's Deep Blue defeating world chess champion Garry Kasparov in 1997 showcased the power of AI in complex strategic decision-making. In recent years, self-driving cars developed by companies like Tesla and Waymo have demonstrated the potential of AI in autonomous transportation. Voice assistants like Amazon's Alexa and Apple's Siri have become part of our daily lives, exemplifying AI's ability to understand and respond to human language.

Conclusion:

The history of AI is a testament to the perseverance, innovation, and collaboration of researchers and scientists over the years. From the early days of AI research to the current era of deep learning and big data, AI has come a long way. Real-life examples illustrate the transformative impact of AI in various domains, and its continued evolution promises to reshape industries, improve healthcare, optimize resource allocation, and drive economic growth. As we delve deeper into this book, we will explore the latest advancements and trends in AI, uncovering the potential and challenges that lie ahead.

CHAPTER 2: KEY CONCEPTS AND TERMINOLOGY IN AI

Introduction:

Artificial Intelligence (AI) is a complex and multidisciplinary field that encompasses a wide range of concepts and terminologies. In this chapter, we will explore the fundamental concepts and terminology in AI, providing a solid foundation for understanding the principles and applications of AI.

1. Machine Learning:

Machine Learning (ML) is a subset of AI that focuses on the development of algorithms and models that enable computers to learn from data and make predictions or take actions without explicit programming. ML algorithms can be broadly categorized into supervised learning, unsupervised learning, and reinforcement learning. Examples of machine learning applications include image recognition, natural language processing, and recommendation systems.

2. Deep Learning:

Deep Learning (DL) is a subfield of machine learning that employs neural networks with multiple layers to model and understand complex patterns in data. Deep learning has achieved remarkable success in various domains, such as computer vision, speech recognition, and natural language processing. Convolutional

Neural Networks (CNNs) and Recurrent Neural Networks (RNNs) are common architectures used in deep learning.

3. Neural Networks:

Neural Networks (NNs) are computational models inspired by the structure and function of the human brain. They consist of interconnected nodes called neurons that process and transmit information. Neural networks can learn and adapt through the adjustment of connection weights. They are the building blocks of deep learning models and have revolutionized the field of AI.

4. Natural Language Processing:

Natural Language Processing (NLP) is a branch of AI that focuses on enabling computers to understand and interact with human language. It involves tasks such as text parsing, sentiment analysis, machine translation, and question-answering systems. NLP techniques have been widely used in applications like virtual assistants, chatbots, and language translation services.

5. Computer Vision:

Computer Vision is a field of AI that focuses on enabling computers to understand and interpret visual information from images or videos. It involves tasks such as image classification, object detection, and image segmentation. Computer vision has found applications in autonomous vehicles, surveillance systems, and medical imaging, among others.

6. Reinforcement Learning:

Reinforcement Learning (RL) is a branch of machine learning concerned with decision-making and learning through interaction with an environment. RL agents learn to take action to maximize a reward signal. This learning paradigm has been successfully applied in domains such as game playing (e.g., AlphaGo) and robotics.

Real-Life Examples:

Real-life examples illustrate the practical applications of these key concepts in AI. For instance, Google's DeepMind developed AlphaGo, an AI system that defeated the world champion Go player, demonstrating the power of deep reinforcement learning. Image recognition algorithms in social media platforms like Facebook automatically tag people in photos, showcasing the capabilities of computer vision. Voice assistants like Amazon's Alexa and Apple's Siri utilize natural language processing techniques to understand and respond to user commands.

Conclusion:

Understanding the key concepts and terminology in AI is essential for grasping the principles and applications of this rapidly evolving field. Machine learning, deep learning, neural networks, natural language processing, computer vision, and reinforcement learning are foundational concepts in AI that drive innovations and advancements in various domains. Real-life examples highlight the impact of these concepts in practical applications, showcasing the transformative potential of AI in our everyday lives. As we progress through this book, we will delve deeper into these concepts and explore their practical implementations and implications.

CHAPTER 3:
MACHINE LEARNING ALGORITHMS AND TECHNIQUES

Introduction:

Machine learning is a subset of artificial intelligence that focuses on developing algorithms and models that enable computers to learn from data and make predictions or take actions without explicit programming. In this chapter, we will explore different machine learning algorithms and techniques, discussing their underlying principles, applications, and real-life examples.

1. Supervised Learning:

Supervised learning is a type of machine learning where the algorithm learns from labelled training data to make predictions or classify new, unseen data. Common supervised learning algorithms include linear regression, logistic regression, decision trees, random forests, support vector machines (SVM), and naive Bayes. These algorithms are used in various applications such as spam filtering, credit scoring, and medical diagnosis.

Real-Life Example: One notable example of supervised learning is the use of machine learning algorithms in email spam detection. By training an algorithm with a labelled dataset of spam and non-spam emails, it can learn to classify incoming emails as either spam or not spam, helping users to filter out unwanted messages.

2. Unsupervised Learning:

Unsupervised learning involves training machine learning algorithms on unlabelled data to identify patterns or structures within the data. Unlike supervised learning, there are no predefined labels or outcomes. Clustering and dimensionality reduction are common unsupervised learning techniques. Clustering algorithms such as k-means and hierarchical clustering group similar data points together, while dimensionality reduction techniques like principal component analysis (PCA) reduce the dimensionality of the data.

Real-Life Example: An example of unsupervised learning is customer segmentation in marketing. By applying clustering algorithms to customer data, businesses can identify distinct groups of customers with similar characteristics or behaviours. This information can then be used to personalize marketing campaigns and tailor product offerings to different customer segments.

3. Reinforcement Learning:

Reinforcement learning involves training an agent to interact with an environment and learn from the feedback it receives. The agent takes actions to maximize a cumulative reward signal over time. Reinforcement learning algorithms, such as Q-learning and deep Q-networks (DQN), have been successfully applied in areas like game playing, robotics, and autonomous driving.

Real-Life Example: One prominent real-life example of reinforcement learning is the training of autonomous vehicles. Through reinforcement learning, autonomous vehicles learn to navigate complex road environments, make decisions, and respond to changing conditions to maximize safety and efficiency.

4. Deep Learning:

Deep learning is a subset of machine learning that utilizes artificial neural networks with multiple layers to learn hierarchical representations of data. Deep learning has achieved remarkable success in domains such as computer vision, natural language processing, and speech recognition. Convolutional neural networks (CNNs) are commonly used in image and video analysis, while recurrent neural networks (RNNs) are effective in sequence-based tasks.

Real-Life Example: A notable example of deep learning is the use of CNNs in image recognition. Deep learning models, such as the ones used in facial recognition technology, have surpassed human-level performance in tasks such as object recognition and image classification.

Conclusion:

Machine learning algorithms and techniques play a crucial role in extracting knowledge and insights from data. Supervised learning algorithms enable accurate predictions and classifications, unsupervised learning techniques help discover patterns and structures in unlabelled data, reinforcement learning allows agents to learn from interactions with the environment, and deep learning models learn hierarchical representations of complex data. Real-life examples demonstrate the practical applications of these machine-learning techniques, showcasing their impact across various domains. As we delve deeper into the book, we will explore these algorithms and techniques in more detail, understanding their strengths, limitations, and practical considerations.

CHAPTER 4: DEEP LEARNING AND NEURAL NETWORKS

Introduction:

Deep learning, a subfield of machine learning, has emerged as a powerful approach to solving complex problems by mimicking the human brain's neural networks. In this chapter, we will delve into the principles, architecture, and applications of deep learning, highlighting the role of neural networks in enabling deep learning algorithms to learn and make predictions from large and diverse datasets.

1. Neural Networks:

Neural networks are the building blocks of deep learning models. They consist of interconnected nodes, or artificial neurons, organized in layers. Each node receives input signals, performs a mathematical computation, and passes the result to the next layer. The layers typically include an input layer, one or more hidden layers, and an output layer. The connections between the neurons have weights that are adjusted during the training process to optimize the model's performance.

Real-Life Example: One prominent example of neural networks in action is image recognition. Convolutional neural networks (CNNs) have revolutionized image classification tasks by automatically learning features directly from the raw image data.

For instance, CNNs have been used to identify objects, recognize faces, and diagnose medical conditions from medical images.

2. Training and Backpropagation:

To train a neural network, a process called backpropagation is used. During training, the network learns to adjust the weights of the connections by comparing its predicted output with the desired output. Backpropagation calculates the gradient of the error concerning the network's weights and updates them accordingly using optimization algorithms such as stochastic gradient descent (SGD).

Real-Life Example: An application of backpropagation is natural language processing. Recurrent neural networks (RNNs) have been employed to generate text and predict the next word in a sequence. By training on large text datasets, RNNs can learn grammar and context, enabling tasks like language translation and sentiment analysis.

3. Deep Learning Architectures:

Deep learning models employ various architectures to tackle different tasks. In addition to CNNs and RNNs, there are other architectures such as generative adversarial networks (GANs) for generating new data, long short-term memory (LSTM) networks for sequence learning, and transformer networks for natural language processing tasks.

Real-Life Example: GANs have found applications in creating realistic images, videos, and audio. For instance, StyleGAN, a variant of GAN, has been used to generate lifelike human faces that are indistinguishable from real photographs. This technology has implications in gaming, virtual reality, and entertainment industries.

4. Deep Learning Applications:

Deep learning has revolutionized various fields, including

computer vision, natural language processing, speech recognition, and healthcare. It has achieved breakthroughs in image classification, object detection, speech synthesis, and language translation, among others. Deep learning models have also been employed in autonomous vehicles, drug discovery, and financial prediction.

Real-Life Example: Self-driving cars rely on deep learning models for perception tasks, such as detecting and recognizing objects on the road, interpreting traffic signs, and predicting pedestrian behaviour. These models enable the vehicle to make real-time decisions based on input from sensors and cameras, ensuring safe navigation.

Conclusion:

Deep learning, powered by neural networks, has propelled advancements in machine learning, enabling computers to learn and make predictions from complex and diverse datasets. Neural networks, with their interconnected nodes and adjustable weights, form the backbone of deep learning models. Through training and backpropagation, these models optimize their performance. Deep learning architectures, including CNNs, RNNs, GANs, and transformers, address specific tasks and have revolutionized image recognition, natural language processing, and generative modelling. Real-life examples demonstrate the impact of deep learning across various domains, from healthcare and autonomous vehicles to entertainment and finance. As deep learning continues to evolve, it holds immense potential for solving complex problems and driving innovation in diverse industries.

CHAPTER 5: NATURAL LANGUAGE PROCESSING AND UNDERSTANDING

Introduction:

Natural Language Processing (NLP) is a field of artificial intelligence that focuses on the interaction between computers and human language. It involves the development of algorithms and models that enable computers to understand, interpret, and generate human language in a way that is meaningful and useful. In this chapter, we will explore the key concepts, techniques, and applications of NLP.

1. Fundamentals of Natural Language Processing:

NLP involves several fundamental tasks, including text tokenization, part-of-speech tagging, syntactic parsing, named entity recognition, and sentiment analysis. These tasks help break down and analyse the structure and meaning of the text, enabling machines to process and understand human language.

Real-Life Example: Chatbots and virtual assistants, such as Amazon's Alexa and Apple's Siri, rely on NLP techniques to understand user queries and provide relevant responses. By analysing the input text, these systems can extract intent, entities, and context to deliver accurate and contextualized information or perform specific tasks.

2. Language Modelling and Text Generation:

Language modelling is a crucial component of NLP, aiming to predict the next word or sequence of words given a context. It utilizes techniques such as n-gram models, recurrent neural networks (RNNs), and transformers to generate coherent and contextually appropriate text.

Real-Life Example: Language models have been utilized to generate realistic and human-like text in various applications, including automated content creation, chatbot responses, and even creative writing. Open Ai's GPT-3 model has demonstrated impressive capabilities in generating coherent and contextually relevant text across a wide range of topics.

3. Machine Translation:

Machine translation is an essential application of NLP, enabling the automated translation of text from one language to another. It employs techniques such as statistical machine translation, neural machine translation, and transformer models to achieve accurate and fluent translations.

Real-Life Example: Google Translate is a prime example of machine translation in action. By applying sophisticated NLP algorithms and machine learning techniques, it allows users to translate text and even entire documents between multiple languages, breaking down language barriers and facilitating communication.

4. Sentiment Analysis and Opinion Mining:

Sentiment analysis involves determining the sentiment or emotional tone expressed in a piece of text, such as positive, negative, or neutral. It helps businesses gauge public opinion, analyse customer feedback, and monitor social media sentiment towards their products or services.

Real-Life Example: Social media platforms employ sentiment analysis to understand the sentiment of user posts and comments. For instance, Twitter uses sentiment analysis to categorize tweets as positive, negative, or neutral, allowing users and businesses to gauge public opinion on various topics and products.

5. Question Answering and Information Extraction:

NLP techniques can be applied to extract relevant information from text and provide accurate answers to user queries. Question-answering systems leverage natural language understanding to comprehend questions and retrieve relevant information from large knowledge bases or text corpora.

Real-Life Example: IBM's Watson, a question-answering system, gained prominence when it competed on the quiz show Jeopardy! in 2011. Watson's ability to understand natural language questions and retrieve precise answers from vast amounts of information showcased the potential of NLP in question answering and information extraction.

Conclusion:

Natural Language Processing plays a pivotal role in enabling machines to understand, interpret, and generate human language. It encompasses various tasks, including text tokenization, part-of-speech tagging, syntactic parsing, sentiment analysis, and machine translation. Real-life applications of NLP can be seen in chatbots, language generation models, machine translation systems, sentiment analysis tools, and question-answering systems. As NLP continues to advance, it holds immense potential in revolutionizing communication, information retrieval, customer service, and decision-making across industries.

PART II: EXPLORING GPT AND ITS APPLICATIONS.

CHAPTER 6: UNDERSTANDING GENERATIVE PRE-TRAINED TRANSFORMERS (GPT)

Introduction:

Generative Pre-trained Transformers (GPT) are a class of deep learning models that have gained significant attention in the field of natural language processing (NLP). These models, developed by Open AI, have shown remarkable capabilities in generating coherent and contextually relevant text. In this chapter, we will explore the key concepts, architecture, and applications of GPT models.

1. The Transformer Architecture:

GPT models are based on the Transformer architecture, which revolutionized the field of NLP. The Transformer consists of an encoder-decoder structure with attention mechanisms that allow the model to focus on relevant parts of the input text and generate output with contextual understanding.

Real-Life Example: One prominent application of the Transformer architecture is Google's BERT (Bidirectional Encoder Representations from Transformers), which has significantly improved the performance of various NLP tasks, including sentiment analysis, named entity recognition and question answering.

2. Pre-training and Fine-tuning:

GPT models are pre-trained on large amounts of text data to learn the statistical patterns and relationships present in the language. This pre-training phase involves unsupervised learning, where the model predicts missing words or sentences in each context. After pre-training, the model is fine-tuned on specific tasks with labelled data to adapt to specific applications.

Real-Life Example: Open Ai's GPT-3, one of the most powerful GPT models, was pre-trained on a vast corpus of internet text data, consisting of books, articles, and websites. This pre-training allowed the model to learn grammar, semantics, and the world knowledge required for generating coherent and contextually appropriate text.

3. Text Generation and Completion:

GPT models excel in text generation tasks, allowing them to generate human-like text based on a given prompt or context. By leveraging the learned patterns and relationships from the pre-training phase, the models can produce coherent and contextually relevant sentences, paragraphs, or even entire articles.

Real-Life Example: GPT models have been used to generate creative writing, news articles, product reviews, and chatbot responses. For instance, AI Dungeon, a text-based adventure game, utilizes GPT-3 to generate dynamic and interactive narratives based on user inputs.

4. Language Understanding and Contextual Reasoning:

GPT models demonstrate a strong ability to understand and reason about the context of the input text. They can capture subtle nuances, disambiguate word meanings, and maintain coherence throughout the generated text, making them useful for tasks that require understanding and manipulation of language.

Real-Life Example: GPT models have been applied to chatbots and virtual assistants to provide more natural and contextually appropriate responses. These models can understand user queries, extract relevant information, and generate informative and engaging responses.

5. Ethical Considerations and Limitations:

As with any powerful technology, GPT models raise ethical concerns, such as the potential for misinformation, biased language generation, and misuse for malicious purposes. Researchers and developers must be vigilant in addressing these concerns and implementing safeguards to ensure the responsible use of GPT models.

Real-Life Example: In 2020, OpenAI withheld the release of the full GPT-3 model, citing concerns about its potential misuse in generating deceptive or harmful content. This decision highlights the importance of responsible development and deployment of AI models.

Conclusion:

Generative Pre-trained Transformers (GPT) models have revolutionized the field of natural language processing by enabling the generation of coherent and contextually relevant text. These models, based on the Transformer architecture, leverage pre-training and fine-tuning to learn the statistical patterns and relationships in language. GPT models have a wide range of applications, including text generation, language understanding, and contextual reasoning. However, ethical considerations and limitations must be carefully addressed to ensure the responsible and beneficial use of these powerful models in real-world scenarios. As GPT models continue to evolve, they hold the potential to shape various aspects of human-machine interaction, content generation, and information retrieval in the future.

CHAPTER 7: GPT ARCHITECTURES AND VARIANTS

Introduction:

In Chapter 6, we explored the fundamentals of Generative Pre-trained Transformers (GPT) and their applications. In this chapter, we will delve deeper into the different architectures and variants of GPT models. These variations have been developed to address specific challenges and improve the performance of the original GPT models. We will discuss the key features, advantages, and real-life examples of these architectures.

1. GPT-2: Scaling Up Performance:

GPT-2 is an enhanced version of the original GPT model that introduced larger model sizes and more training data. With up to 1.5 billion parameters, GPT-2 exhibits improved performance in various language tasks, including text generation, language understanding, and question answering.

Real-Life Example: OpenAI's GPT-2 model gained attention for its ability to generate highly realistic and coherent text. It has been used for creative writing, content generation, and even creating fake news articles.

2. GPT-3: Unleashing Unprecedented Power:

GPT-3 is the largest and most powerful GPT model to date, with a staggering 175 billion parameters. This massive scale allows GPT-3 to excel in a wide range of language tasks and highly generate context-aware and nuanced text.

Real-Life Example: OpenAI's GPT-3 has been used to develop language translation systems, chatbots, and virtual assistants that can provide detailed and accurate responses to user queries.

3. GPT-Neo: Open-Source Community Effort:

GPT-Neo is an open-source project that aims to replicate the capabilities of GPT models with a smaller computational footprint. This initiative focuses on creating more accessible and resource efficient GPT models, allowing researchers and developers to leverage the power of GPT without the need for large-scale computing resources.

Real-Life Example: Hugging Face, a popular open-source library, developed a GPT-Neo variant known as "gpt-2.7B," which is a more computationally efficient version of GPT-2. This model has been widely used by the research community for various natural language processing tasks.

4. GPT-3 Finetuning: Customization for Specific Tasks:

While GPT models are pre-trained on a large corpus of text, they can also be fine-tuned on specific datasets to perform well on tasks. By fine-tuning, developers can customize the model's behaviour and optimize its performance for specific applications.

Real-Life Example: ChatGPT, a variant of GPT-3, was fine-tuned by OpenAI to be a chatbot specifically designed to engage in human-like conversations. It has been integrated into various customer support systems, providing efficient and interactive customer service.

Conclusion:

The evolution of GPT models has led to various architectures and variants, each with its strengths and characteristics. GPT-2 introduced larger model sizes, enhancing the performance of text generation, and understanding tasks. GPT-3, with its unprecedented scale, unlocked new possibilities and achieved remarkable results across a wide range of language-related applications. GPT-Neo represents a community-driven effort to make GPT models more accessible and computationally efficient. Additionally, the ability to fine-tune GPT models allows for customization and optimization for specific tasks.

Real-life examples demonstrate the practical utility of GPT architectures and variants. They have been employed in creative writing, content generation, customer support, and other language-based applications. These models have shown impressive capabilities in understanding context, generating coherent text, and engaging in human-like conversations.

As GPT models continue to evolve, it is crucial to consider ethical considerations and address challenges related to bias, misinformation, and misuse. Responsible development and deployment of GPT architectures and variants are necessary to ensure their beneficial and ethical use in real-world scenarios. The advancements in GPT models have opened new horizons in natural language processing and have the potential to transform various industries, including education, healthcare, and communication, in the years to come.

CHAPTER 8: GPT IN LANGUAGE GENERATION AND TEXT SUMMARISATION

1. Language Generation with GPT:

GPT models have revolutionized the field of language generation, enabling the production of coherent and contextually relevant text. By leveraging the vast amounts of pre-training data, GPT models can generate paragraphs, essays, stories, and even poetry naturally and engagingly.

Real-Life Example: OpenAI's GPT-3 has been used to develop AI-based content generation platforms, such as article writing assistants, creative writing tools, and story generators. These applications empower users to effortlessly generate high-quality text content for various purposes, saving time and effort.

2. Text Summarization with GPT:

GPT models have also proven to be effective in text summarization tasks, where the objective is to condense longer documents into shorter, coherent summaries. By understanding the context and salient information, GPT models can generate concise and informative summaries that capture the essence of the original text.

Real-Life Example: Summarization algorithms powered by GPT have been used in news aggregation platforms and content curation systems. These systems can analyse and summarize large volumes of articles, enabling users to quickly grasp the main points and stay updated on current events.

3. Challenges and Considerations:

While GPT models have demonstrated impressive language generation and summarization capabilities, there are some challenges and considerations to keep in mind. One major challenge is the potential for generating biased or misleading content. GPT models are trained on large datasets that may contain inherent biases, and if not properly addressed, these biases can be reflected in the generated text. Ensuring fairness and accuracy in the output requires careful curation of training data and ongoing monitoring.

Another consideration is the need for fine-tuning and customization. GPT models are pre-trained on generic datasets and may not be optimized for specific domains or tasks. Fine-tuning the models with domain-specific data can improve their performance and relevance in specific contexts.

4. Real-Life Applications:

GPT models have been deployed in various real-life applications that rely on language generation and text summarization. For example, AI-powered virtual assistants can utilize GPT models to provide detailed responses to user queries or generate informative text-based responses in chat interfaces.

In the news industry, GPT-powered systems can automatically generate concise news summaries that provide readers with a quick overview of articles, helping them navigate through large volumes of information more efficiently.

Conclusion:

The application of GPT models in language generation and text summarization has opened new possibilities in content creation, creative writing, and information retrieval. These models have the potential to streamline workflows, improve productivity, and enhance user experiences in various domains.

Real-life examples demonstrate how GPT-powered platforms and systems have been employed in content generation, creative writing, and news aggregation. By leveraging the power of GPT, users can generate high-quality text content, access informative summaries, and stay informed in an increasingly data-rich world.

While GPT models offer immense potential, addressing challenges related to bias, accuracy, and fine-tuning remains crucial. Responsible use and continuous refinement of these models are essential to ensure ethical and trustworthy language generation and text summarization systems.

As GPT models continue to evolve and improve, we can expect further advancements in language generation and text summarization, empowering individuals, and organizations to effectively communicate, summarize information, and make sense of the vast amounts of text data available.

CHAPTER 9: GPT IN IMAGE AND VIDEO PROCESSING

Introduction:

In this chapter, we explore the fascinating applications of Generative Pre-trained Transformers (GPT) in the field of image and video processing. While GPT models are primarily known for their text-generation capabilities, they have also demonstrated promising results in generating and manipulating visual content. We will delve into the relevant techniques, discuss real-life examples, and examine the impact of GPT in this domain.

1. GPT for Image Generation:

GPT models have shown remarkable abilities in generating realistic and diverse images. By conditioning the models on specific prompts or seed images, GPT can generate new images that resemble the input data. The models learn to capture various visual features, such as shapes, colours, and textures, allowing for the creation of visually appealing and coherent images.

Real-Life Example: OpenAI's DALL-E project utilized GPT-3 to generate unique images based on textual descriptions. The model could generate novel and imaginative images of objects that had never been seen before, showcasing the potential of GPT in image generation.

2. GPT for Image Editing and Manipulation:

GPT models can also be employed for image editing and manipulation tasks. By providing textual instructions or annotations, GPT models can modify existing images to meet specific criteria. This includes altering attributes such as colours, styles, and compositions, enabling users to customize and transform images according to their preferences.

Real-Life Example: GPT-based image editing tools have been developed, allowing users to modify images using natural language instructions. For instance, users can provide textual descriptions like "Make the sky more vibrant" or "Remove the background" to achieve desired image edits automatically.

3. GPT for Video Generation and Editing:

GPT models have shown potential in the generation and editing of videos as well. By extending the techniques used in image generation, GPT can generate video sequences based on textual prompts or seed videos. This opens possibilities for creating dynamic and visually engaging video content.

Real-Life Example: GPT-based video generation has been used in applications such as video game development and special effects in the film industry. By leveraging GPT models, developers and animators can generate lifelike characters, realistic environments, and captivating visual effects.

4. Challenges and Considerations:

While GPT models have shown promising results in image and video processing, several challenges and considerations need to be addressed. One major challenge is the computational complexity of processing visual data. Image and video data are high-dimensional, requiring significant computational resources for training and inference. Additionally, the models need to capture spatial and temporal dependencies accurately to generate realistic visual content.

Another consideration is the need for large and diverse training datasets. GPT models perform best when trained on a wide range of visual data to learn the intricate details and variations present in images and videos.

5. Real-Life Applications:

GPT models have been applied in various real-life scenarios involving image and video processing. In the field of computer vision, GPT-based models have been used for tasks such as image classification, object detection, and semantic segmentation.

In the entertainment industry, GPT-powered systems have been employed for video editing, special effects, and virtual reality experiences. These applications allow content creators to produce visually stunning and immersive media content.

Conclusion:

The application of GPT models in image and video processing has opened new possibilities for content generation, editing, and manipulation. Real-life examples have demonstrated the potential of GPT in generating images, editing visuals, and creating dynamic videos.

While challenges such as computational complexity and dataset requirements exist, advancements in hardware and the availability of diverse training data are mitigating these challenges. As GPT models continue to evolve, we can expect further advancements in image and video processing, enhancing our ability to generate, edit, and manipulate visual content with greater ease and creativity.

CHAPTER 10: GPT IN VOICE RECOGNITION AND VIRTUAL ASSISTANTS

Introduction:

In recent years, voice recognition technology and virtual assistants have become increasingly prevalent in our daily lives. These technologies, powered by advanced natural language processing and AI algorithms, have significantly improved the way we interact with our devices and access information. In this chapter, we will explore the role of Generative Pre-trained Transformers (GPT) in voice recognition and virtual assistants, examining their impact and discussing real-life examples of their applications.

Voice Recognition Technology:

Voice recognition technology refers to the ability of a machine or computer system to understand and interpret spoken language. It involves converting spoken words into text and analysing that text to derive meaning and perform relevant tasks. GPT, with its language generation capabilities and deep learning algorithms, has greatly enhanced the accuracy and efficiency of voice recognition systems.

GPT in Virtual Assistants:

Virtual assistants are AI-driven software programs designed to provide personalized assistance and perform tasks based on voice commands or text inputs. GPT plays a crucial role in enabling virtual assistants to understand and respond to human queries conversationally. By utilizing GPT, virtual assistants can generate natural and contextually relevant responses, creating a more interactive and human-like user experience.

Real-Life Examples:

1. Amazon Alexa:
Amazon's virtual assistant, Alexa, is one of the most widely recognized and utilized voice-activated virtual assistants. Powered by GPT-based algorithms, Alexa can understand and respond to a wide range of user commands, from playing music and setting reminders to controlling smart home devices. The integration of GPT allows Alexa to generate natural and coherent responses, making interactions with the virtual assistant more seamless and intuitive.

2. Apple Siri:
Siri, the virtual assistant developed by Apple, relies on GPT technology to process voice commands, and provide intelligent responses. Siri can perform various tasks, such as sending messages, making calls, and providing information on weather, sports, and news. GPT algorithms enable Siri to understand user inputs and generate appropriate and contextually relevant responses, enhancing the user experience.

3. Google Assistant:
Google Assistant is another prominent virtual assistant that utilizes GPT to understand and respond to user queries. Google Assistant can perform tasks such as answering questions, providing directions, and making reservations. By leveraging GPT, Google Assistant can process and interpret user inputs accurately, generating informative and helpful responses.

Benefits and Challenges:

The integration of GPT in voice recognition and virtual assistants offers several benefits. Firstly, it enables more accurate speech recognition, leading to improved user experiences and fewer errors in understanding user commands. GPT also enhances the conversational abilities of virtual assistants, making interactions more natural and engaging. Additionally, GPT-based virtual assistants can adapt to individual user preferences, providing personalized and tailored responses.

However, there are also challenges associated with GPT in voice recognition and virtual assistants. One significant challenge is ensuring privacy and data security. Virtual assistants need access to a substantial amount of personal data to provide personalized responses, raising concerns about data privacy and protection. Additionally, maintaining transparency and explain ability in GPT algorithms is crucial to address concerns related to biases and potential misuse.

Future Directions:

As GPT continues to advance, voice recognition and virtual assistants are expected to become even more sophisticated. Future developments may include improved speech-to-text accuracy, enhanced contextual understanding, and more natural and human-like responses. Additionally, integrating GPT with other AI technologies, such as computer vision and machine translation, may unlock new possibilities for voice-enabled applications.

Conclusion:
GPT has revolutionized voice recognition technology and virtual assistants, making them more intelligent, interactive, and user-friendly. Through the integration of GPT algorithms, virtual assistants like Amazon Alexa, Apple Siri, and Google Assistant have become integral parts of our daily lives, offering personalized assistance, and streamlining various tasks. As GPT continues to evolve, we can expect voice recognition and virtual assistants to

become even more advanced, enhancing our interactions with technology and transforming the way we access information and accomplish tasks.

PART III:
ADVANCEMENTS
IN AI AND GPT

CHAPTER 11:
REINFORCEMENT LEARNING AND AI AGENTS

Introduction:

Reinforcement Learning (RL) is a subfield of Artificial Intelligence (AI) that focuses on enabling agents to learn and make decisions through interactions with their environment. RL algorithms enable AI agents to learn from trial and error, receive feedback in the form of rewards or penalties, and develop optimal strategies for achieving predefined goals. In this chapter, we will explore the concept of reinforcement learning, discuss its underlying principles, and examine real-life examples of AI agents trained using RL techniques.

1. The Basics of Reinforcement Learning:

Reinforcement learning operates on the principle of an agent interacting with an environment. The agent takes actions, which in turn affect the environment, and receives feedback in the form of rewards or penalties based on the desirability of its actions. The goal of the agent is to maximize the cumulative reward over time by learning a policy—a mapping of states to actions—that leads to optimal decision-making.

2. RL Algorithms and Techniques:

There are several RL algorithms and techniques that enable agents to learn and improve their decision-making abilities. These include:

a. Value-based methods: These algorithms learn the value function, which represents the expected cumulative reward for being in a particular state and taking a specific action. Examples include Q-learning and Deep Q-Networks (DQNs).

b. Policy-based methods: These algorithms directly learn the policy, mapping states to actions, without explicitly estimating the value function. Examples include Policy Gradients and Proximal Policy Optimization (PPO).

c. Actor-Critic methods: These algorithms combine aspects of both value-based and policy-based methods by using a value function and a policy function. Examples include Advantage Actor-Critic (A2C) and Asynchronous Advantage Actor-Critic (A3C).

d. Model-based methods: These algorithms learn a model of the environment, allowing the agent to simulate and plan. Model Predictive Control (MPC) is an example of a model-based RL algorithm.

3. Real-Life Examples:

Reinforcement learning has found applications in various domains, ranging from game playing to robotics and autonomous systems. Here are some notable real-life examples:

a. AlphaGo: Developed by DeepMind, AlphaGo became famous for defeating world-champion Go players. It utilized a combination of RL techniques, including Monte Carlo Tree Search, to learn optimal strategies and make moves in the game.

b. Autonomous Driving: RL has been applied to train self-driving cars to navigate complex road environments. By interacting with the environment and learning from rewards and penalties, AI agents can develop driving policies that prioritize safety and efficiency.

c. Robotics: RL is used to train robotic agents to perform tasks such as grasping objects, walking, or manipulating objects in the physical world. These agents learn through trial and error, improving their skills and adapting to different scenarios.

d. Inventory Management: RL techniques have been applied to optimize inventory management for businesses. By learning from historical data and adjusting ordering policies, AI agents can minimize costs and maintain optimal stock levels.

Conclusion:

Reinforcement learning is a powerful approach that enables AI agents to learn and make decisions through interactions with their environment. By leveraging rewards and penalties, RL algorithms can guide agents towards optimal strategies and goal-oriented behaviours. Real-life examples, such as AlphaGo, autonomous driving, robotics, and inventory management, showcase the practical applications of RL in various domains.

As the field of reinforcement learning continues to advance, we can expect to see more sophisticated AI agents that can solve complex problems and making intelligent decisions in dynamic environments. However, challenges such as sample efficiency, generalization, and safety in RL algorithms remain areas of active research and development.

Overall, reinforcement learning provides a framework for training AI agents to learn from experience and optimize their decision-making processes. It holds immense potential for solving real-world problems and advancing the capabilities of AI systems across different industries.

CHAPTER 12: EXPLAIN ABILITY AND ETHICAL CONSIDERATIONS IN AI

Introduction:

As Artificial Intelligence (AI) continues to advance and permeate various aspects of our lives, there is a growing need to understand and address the issues of explain ability and ethics. In this chapter, we will explore the importance of explain ability in AI systems, discuss the ethical considerations surrounding AI, and examine real-life examples where these issues have come into play.

1. The Importance of Explain ability:

Explain ability refers to the ability to understand and interpret how AI systems arrive at their decisions or recommendations. It is crucial for building trust, accountability, and transparency in AI systems. When users, stakeholders, or regulatory bodies can comprehend the reasoning behind AI-generated outcomes, it enables them to assess the system's reliability, detect biases, and identify potential risks.

2. Explain ability Techniques:

There are various techniques and approaches to achieving explain ability in AI systems. Some common methods include:

a. Rule-based explanations: AI systems can provide explanations in the form of if-then rules, which make the decision-making process more interpretable and understandable.

b. Feature importance and relevance: By identifying the features or variables that contribute most to the AI system's decision, explanations can be generated to highlight the key factors influencing the outcomes.

c. Model-agnostic methods: These approaches aim to explain the behaviour of any AI model, regardless of its underlying architecture or algorithm. Techniques like LIME (Local Interpretable Model-Agnostic Explanations) provide post-hoc explanations by approximating the behaviour of the AI model locally.

3. Ethical Considerations in AI:

As AI becomes increasingly integrated into society, ethical considerations arise. It is essential to ensure that AI systems are designed and deployed in a manner that aligns with societal values and principles. Some key ethical considerations include:

a. Bias and fairness: AI systems can inadvertently perpetuate biases present in the data they are trained on. It is crucial to address these biases and strive for fairness in decision-making processes to avoid discriminatory outcomes.

b. Privacy and data protection: AI systems often require access to sensitive data. Ensuring proper privacy protection and complying with data protection regulations is vital to safeguard individuals' rights and maintain trust.

c. Accountability and responsibility: Clear accountability mechanisms should be in place to attribute responsibility for the actions and decisions made by AI systems. This includes defining roles and responsibilities for system developers, users, and other stakeholders.

4. Real-Life Examples:

Real-life examples demonstrate the importance of explain ability and ethical considerations in AI:

a. Facial Recognition Technology: Facial recognition systems have faced scrutiny due to concerns of bias and invasion of privacy. In some instances, these systems have been found to have higher error rates when identifying individuals from certain racial or ethnic groups, highlighting the need for transparency and fairness.

b. Credit Scoring Algorithms: Algorithms used in credit scoring can significantly impact individuals' financial opportunities. Ensuring fairness and transparency in these algorithms is crucial to avoid discriminatory lending practices.

c. Autonomous Vehicles: The development of autonomous vehicles raises ethical questions, such as how AI systems should prioritize human safety in potential accident scenarios. Public discussion and consensus are needed to determine the ethical principles that should guide these decisions.

Conclusion:

Explain ability and ethical considerations are integral components of responsible AI development and deployment. By ensuring transparency, addressing biases, and upholding ethical principles, we can foster trust and accountability in AI systems. Real-life examples, such as facial recognition technology, credit scoring algorithms, and autonomous vehicles, demonstrate the relevance and impact of explain ability and ethical considerations in AI.

As AI continues to advance, it is crucial to have ongoing discussions and collaborations among researchers, policymakers, and society at large to establish guidelines, regulations, and ethical frameworks. This will help ensure that AI technologies are developed and used in ways that benefit humanity while upholding fundamental values such as fairness, privacy, and accountability. Ultimately, a thoughtful and responsible approach to explain ability and ethics in AI will contribute to the positive impact and acceptance of AI in our society.

CHAPTER 13: TRANSFER LEARNING AND DOMAIN ADAPTATION

Introduction:

Transfer learning and domain adaptation are two essential concepts in the field of Artificial Intelligence (AI) and Machine Learning (ML). In this chapter, we will explore how these techniques enable the transfer of knowledge and skills from one domain to another, allowing AI models to leverage pre-existing knowledge and adapt to new environments. We will discuss the relevance of transfer learning and domain adaptation in real-world applications and provide examples that highlight their benefits and challenges.

1. Transfer Learning:

Transfer learning involves utilizing knowledge learned from one task or domain to improve performance on a different but related task or domain. Instead of training a model from scratch, transfer learning leverages pre-trained models that have learned representations from large-scale datasets. This approach significantly reduces the need for extensive labelled data and computational resources.

2. Real-Life Examples:

a. Image Recognition: In the field of computer vision, transfer learning has been widely used for image recognition tasks. For example, models pre-trained on ImageNet, a large dataset with millions of labelled images, can be fine-tuned for specific image recognition tasks such as identifying objects or classifying images in different domains such as medical imaging or satellite imagery.

b. Natural Language Processing: Transfer learning has also found applications in natural language processing tasks. For instance, models pre-trained on large text corpora, such as OpenAI's GPT models, can be fine-tuned for specific tasks like sentiment analysis, question answering, or language translation. This approach enables faster and more accurate development of NLP models for various domains.

3. Domain Adaptation:

Domain adaptation focuses on adapting a model trained on a source domain to perform well on a target domain with different characteristics. It addresses the challenge of transferring knowledge when there is a distribution shift between the training and testing data. Domain adaptation techniques aim to bridge this gap and minimize the performance degradation caused by the domain shift.

4. Real-Life Examples:

a. Speech Recognition: Domain adaptation is crucial in speech recognition systems, where the acoustic characteristics of speech can vary across different environments. Techniques such as unsupervised domain adaptation and adversarial domain adaptation have been used to adapt speech recognition models trained on clean data to perform well in noisy or acoustically challenging environments.

b. Autonomous Driving: Autonomous driving systems need to

adapt to various road and weather conditions. Domain adaptation enables these systems to generalize their knowledge learned from one set of conditions to perform well in different scenarios, such as transitioning from a training environment to real-world driving conditions.

Conclusion:

Transfer learning and domain adaptation are powerful techniques that enable AI models to leverage pre-existing knowledge and adapt to new domains and environments. These approaches have proven effective in various real-world applications, including image recognition, natural language processing, speech recognition, and autonomous driving. By transferring knowledge and adapting models to new tasks and domains, we can overcome data limitations, reduce training time, and improve performance in diverse scenarios.

However, challenges exist in effectively applying transfer learning and domain adaptation, such as addressing domain discrepancies, selecting appropriate source domains, and managing the trade-off between transferred knowledge and task-specific learning. Ongoing research and development in these areas are crucial to further enhance the effectiveness and applicability of transfer learning and domain adaptation techniques.

As AI continues to advance, transfer learning and domain adaptation will play an increasingly vital role in enabling AI systems to generalize knowledge and adapt to new contexts. These techniques pave the way for more efficient and effective AI solutions, addressing real-world challenges across various domains and improving the overall performance and versatility of AI applications.

CHAPTER 14: FEDERATED LEARNING AND PRIVACY-PRESERVING AI

Introduction:

In the era of big data and privacy concerns, the need for privacy-preserving AI techniques has become paramount. Federated learning is an emerging approach that enables the training of AI models on decentralized data while maintaining data privacy. In this chapter, we will delve into the concept of federated learning and explore its applications, benefits, challenges, and real-life examples.

1. Federated Learning:

Federated learning is a distributed learning paradigm that allows multiple parties to collaboratively train a shared AI model without sharing their raw data. Instead, the training occurs locally on each participant's device or server. The model's updates are then aggregated to create a global model, which is shared among the participants. This approach ensures data privacy as sensitive data remains on the local devices or servers.

2. Real-Life Examples:

a. Mobile Devices: Federated learning has gained traction in mobile applications where user data privacy is crucial. For example, Google implemented federated learning in its Board keyboard app to improve text prediction capabilities. Instead of sending user keystrokes to a centralized server, the model is trained locally on users' devices, and only the model updates are sent to improve the global model. This preserves user privacy while enhancing the app's functionality.

b. Healthcare: Federated learning has shown promise in the healthcare sector, where privacy regulations and data security are of utmost importance. For instance, researchers have explored federated learning for training AI models on medical data from different hospitals. By keeping the data decentralized and training locally, healthcare institutions can collaborate to develop robust models while safeguarding patient privacy.

3. Privacy-Preserving Techniques:

Federated learning incorporates various privacy-preserving techniques to ensure data security and privacy during the training process. Some notable techniques include:

a. Differential Privacy: Differential privacy adds noise to the model updates to protect individual data privacy. By obscuring specific details, it prevents the extraction of sensitive information from the model updates.

b. Secure Aggregation: Secure aggregation protocols allow participants to aggregate their model updates without exposing individual contributions. This ensures that participants' data remains confidential even during the aggregation phase.

4. Benefits and Challenges:

Federated learning offers several benefits, including:

a. Data Privacy: Participants retain control over their data, reducing privacy concerns associated with centralized data storage.

b. Collaboration: Organizations can collaborate and share knowledge without sharing sensitive data.

However, federated learning also poses challenges:

a. Heterogeneous Data: Training models on decentralized data from various sources may introduce distributional disparities and require additional techniques to address the domain shift.

b. Communication Efficiency: Federated learning involves communication between participants, which can be bandwidth-intensive, especially in resource-constrained environments.

Conclusion:

Federated learning is an innovative approach that enables privacy-preserving AI, allowing organizations and individuals to collaborate on training AI models without compromising data privacy. Real-life applications, such as mobile devices and healthcare, have demonstrated the effectiveness of federated learning in maintaining data privacy while improving AI capabilities. Privacy-preserving techniques like differential privacy and secure aggregation play a crucial role in ensuring the confidentiality of participant data.

As privacy concerns continue to grow in the AI landscape, federated learning provides a promising solution for organizations and individuals seeking to leverage the power of AI while preserving data privacy. Future advancements in federated learning techniques, such as addressing heterogeneous data challenges and improving communication efficiency, will further enhance its applicability across diverse domains. With federated learning and privacy-preserving AI, we can strike a balance between data utility and privacy, fostering trust and enabling collaborative AI development in a privacy-conscious world.

CHAPTER 15: AI IN HEALTHCARE AND MEDICINE

Introduction:

Artificial intelligence (AI) has made significant advancements in various industries, and one of its most promising applications is in healthcare and medicine. In this chapter, we will explore the impact of AI in healthcare, its benefits, challenges, and real-life examples of AI integration in medical practices.

1. AI-Assisted Diagnosis and Treatment:

AI algorithms have demonstrated great potential in assisting healthcare professionals with accurate diagnosis and treatment decisions. For example, AI-powered image recognition systems can analyse medical images such as X-rays, CT scans, and MRIs to detect abnormalities or assist in diagnosing conditions like cancer or cardiovascular diseases. These algorithms can process large amounts of data, identify patterns, and provide insights that aid in more precise and timely diagnoses.

Real-Life Example: IBM's Watson for Oncology is an AI system that assists doctors in personalized cancer treatment recommendations by analysing patient data, medical records, and scientific literature. It helps oncologists make evidence-based decisions, improving patient outcomes and streamlining the treatment process.

2. Predictive Analytics and Early Detection:

AI algorithms can analyse vast amounts of patient data, including medical records, genetics, lifestyle factors, and environmental information, to identify patterns and predict disease risks. This enables proactive interventions and early detection of diseases, potentially saving lives and reducing healthcare costs. For instance, AI algorithms can predict the likelihood of developing chronic conditions like diabetes or heart disease, allowing healthcare providers to offer targeted preventive measures.

Real-Life Example: Google's DeepMind developed an AI algorithm that predicts the likelihood of acute kidney injury in hospital patients. By analysing patient data, the algorithm identifies individuals at high risk of developing kidney injury, enabling timely interventions to prevent or mitigate the condition.

3. Drug Discovery and Development:

AI is revolutionizing the process of drug discovery by accelerating the identification and development of potential new drugs. Machine learning algorithms can analyse large datasets, including genetic information and molecular structures, to identify promising drug candidates. This helps researchers streamline the drug development process, reducing the time and costs associated with traditional approaches.

Real-Life Example: Insilico Medicine, an AI-driven drug discovery company, used machine learning algorithms to design a new potential drug candidate for fibrosis. The AI system analysed molecular data and proposed a molecule with a high likelihood of being an effective treatment, which is now undergoing further testing.

4. Personalized Medicine and Precision Healthcare:

AI enables personalized medicine by considering individual variations in genetics, lifestyle, and other factors to tailor treatment plans. Machine learning algorithms can analyse patient data and provide personalized treatment recommendations, improving patient outcomes and reducing adverse reactions. Additionally, AI can help optimize treatment plans by considering factors like drug interactions and patient response predictions.

Real-Life Example: Owkin, a healthcare AI company, developed an algorithm that predicts patient response to cancer treatments by analysing genomics and clinical data. This allows oncologists to choose the most effective treatment options for individual patients, improving treatment outcomes and reducing unnecessary side effects.

Conclusion:

AI has the potential to revolutionize healthcare and medicine, enabling more accurate diagnoses, proactive interventions, efficient drug development, and personalized treatment plans. Real-life examples, such as Watson for Oncology, DeepMind's acute kidney injury prediction algorithm, Insilico Medicine's drug discovery, and Owkin's personalized cancer treatment predictions, demonstrate the transformative impact of AI in healthcare.

However, the integration of AI in healthcare comes with challenges, including data privacy and security, regulatory considerations, ethical concerns, and the need for proper validation and interpretation of AI-generated results. Overcoming these challenges requires collaboration between AI experts, healthcare professionals, policymakers, and regulatory bodies to ensure safe, ethical, and effective AI integration.

As AI continues to advance, it holds great promise in improving patient outcomes, enhancing precision healthcare, and transforming the healthcare industry. By leveraging AI's capabilities, we can achieve more accurate diagnoses, earlier disease detection, and personalized treatment plans, ultimately leading to better healthcare outcomes and improved quality of life for patients.

CHAPTER 16: AI IN FINANCE AND INVESTMENT

Introduction:

Artificial intelligence (AI) has emerged as a powerful tool in the finance and investment industry, revolutionizing how financial institutions operate and make decisions. In this chapter, we will explore the various applications of AI in finance, its benefits, challenges, and real-life examples of AI implementation in financial services.

1. Risk Assessment and Fraud Detection:

AI algorithms can analyse large volumes of financial data, including transaction records, market trends, and customer profiles, to identify patterns and detect potential risks or fraudulent activities. Machine learning algorithms can detect anomalies, unusual patterns, and suspicious behaviour in real-time, enabling financial institutions to take proactive measures to mitigate risks and prevent fraud.

Real-Life Example: PayPal uses AI algorithms to detect and prevent fraudulent transactions by analysing various factors, such as transaction history, user behaviour, and device information. These algorithms can identify and block potentially fraudulent transactions, ensuring secure and reliable payment services.

2. Algorithmic Trading and Portfolio Management:

AI algorithms are widely used in algorithmic trading, where computers make trading decisions based on predefined rules and real-time market data. These algorithms can analyse market trends, historical data, and other relevant factors to execute trades at high speeds and with precision. Additionally, AI can assist in portfolio management by analysing market conditions and recommending optimal asset allocation strategies.

Real-Life Example: Renaissance Technologies' Medallion Fund, one of the most successful hedge funds, utilizes AI-based strategies for high-frequency trading. The fund's algorithms analyse vast amounts of financial data to identify profitable trading opportunities, leading to exceptional returns for investors.

3. Customer Service and Personalized Banking:

AI-powered chatbots and virtual assistants are transforming customer service in the finance industry. These intelligent systems can interact with customers, answer inquiries, provide personalized recommendations, and assist with basic financial transactions. By leveraging natural language processing and machine learning, AI chatbots enhance customer experience and streamline routine tasks.

Real-Life Example: Bank of America's virtual assistant, Erica, uses AI algorithms to provide personalized financial guidance and assistance to customers. Erica can help with tasks like checking account balances, paying bills, and providing personalized spending insights, offering customers a convenient and tailored banking experience.

4. Credit Scoring and Loan Underwriting:

AI algorithms can analyse vast amounts of data, including credit history, income levels, and other relevant factors, to assess creditworthiness and make accurate loan decisions. By leveraging machine learning, AI models can predict the likelihood of loan defaults, assess risk profiles, and streamline the loan underwriting process.

Real-Life Example: LendingClub, an online lending platform, uses AI algorithms to assess borrowers' creditworthiness. The platform analyses various data points to generate a borrower's credit score, helping investors make informed decisions about lending money on the platform.

Conclusion:

AI has revolutionized the finance and investment industry, enabling more accurate risk assessment, fraud detection, algorithmic trading, personalized banking, and efficient credit scoring. Real-life examples, such as PayPal's fraud detection system, Renaissance Technologies' Medallion Fund, Bank of America's virtual assistant Erica, and LendingClub's credit scoring algorithms, showcase the transformative impact of AI in finance.

However, the integration of AI in finance comes with challenges, including data privacy, regulatory compliance, ethical considerations, and the need for human oversight to ensure accountability and transparency. Overcoming these challenges requires collaboration between AI experts, financial institutions, regulators, and policymakers to establish responsible AI frameworks.

As AI continues to advance, it holds great promise in improving risk management, customer service, investment strategies, and overall efficiency in the finance and investment industry. By harnessing the power of AI, financial institutions can enhance decision-making, streamline operations, and deliver more personalized and secure financial services to their customers.

CHAPTER 17: AI IN MANUFACTURING AND INDUSTRY 4.0

Introduction:

The integration of artificial intelligence (AI) in manufacturing has given rise to the concept of Industry 4.0, where advanced technologies revolutionize the way products are manufactured, monitored, and optimized. In this chapter, we will explore the applications of AI in manufacturing and its impact on productivity, efficiency, and innovation. We will also discuss real-life examples that highlight the transformative power of AI in the manufacturing sector.

1. Predictive Maintenance:

AI-powered systems can analyse real-time data from sensors and equipment to detect anomalies, identify potential failures, and predict maintenance needs. By leveraging machine learning algorithms, manufacturers can move from reactive to proactive maintenance strategies, minimizing downtime, optimizing maintenance schedules, and reducing costs.

Real-Life Example: General Electric (GE) uses AI algorithms to predict equipment failure in their jet engines. By continuously monitoring sensor data, AI models can identify signs of potential failure and trigger maintenance actions before major issues occur, ensuring the safe and reliable operation of the engines.

2. Quality Control and Defect Detection:

AI algorithms can analyse images, sensor data, and other relevant inputs to identify defects, inconsistencies, or anomalies in manufacturing processes. By automatically detecting and flagging quality issues, manufacturers can reduce waste, improve product quality, and optimize production efficiency.

Real-Life Example: BMW implemented AI-based quality control systems in their production lines. AI algorithms analyse images of car parts to identify defects or imperfections, ensuring that only high-quality components are used in the assembly process.

3. Supply Chain Optimization:

AI can optimize supply chain operations by analysing large volumes of data, including demand forecasts, inventory levels, transportation logistics, and market trends. By leveraging AI-driven algorithms, manufacturers can optimize inventory management, reduce lead times, and improve overall supply chain efficiency.

Real-Life Example: Amazon utilizes AI algorithms to optimize its warehouse operations and delivery processes. AI-driven systems analyse data on customer orders, inventory levels, and transportation routes to improve order fulfilment, reduce shipping times, and enhance customer satisfaction.

4. Autonomous Robotics and Cobots:

AI-powered robotics and collaborative robots (cobots) are revolutionizing manufacturing processes by performing complex tasks with precision, speed, and flexibility. These robotic systems can work alongside human workers, enhancing productivity, ensuring worker safety, and enabling the automation of repetitive and labour-intensive tasks.

Real-Life Example: Tesla's Gigafactory uses autonomous robots to assemble and transport car components on the production line. These robots work collaboratively with human workers, increasing efficiency and accelerating the manufacturing process.

Conclusion:

The integration of AI in manufacturing and the adoption of Industry 4.0 principles are reshaping the industry, leading to increased productivity, improved product quality, and optimized supply chain operations. Real-life examples, such as GE's predictive maintenance systems, BMW's AI-based quality control, Amazon's supply chain optimization, and Tesla's use of autonomous robots, demonstrate the significant impact of AI on manufacturing processes.

However, the implementation of AI in manufacturing comes with challenges, including data security, ethical considerations, and the need for upskilling the workforce to adapt to new roles. Addressing these challenges requires collaboration between AI experts, manufacturers, policymakers, and workers' organizations to ensure responsible and sustainable integration of AI technologies.

As AI continues to advance, its applications in manufacturing are expected to expand further, enabling increased automation, optimization of production processes, and the development of smart factories. By harnessing the power of AI, manufacturers can unlock new opportunities for innovation, enhance efficiency, and remain competitive in the ever-evolving global marketplace.

CHAPTER 18: AI IN TRANSPORTATION AND AUTONOMOUS VEHICLES

Introduction:

Artificial intelligence (AI) is revolutionizing the transportation industry, paving the way for safer, more efficient, and sustainable modes of transportation. In this chapter, we will explore the applications of AI in transportation, with a specific focus on autonomous vehicles. We will discuss how AI is reshaping the transportation landscape, the benefits it offers, and the challenges that arise with its implementation. Real-life examples will be provided to illustrate the transformative impact of AI in the transportation sector.

1. Autonomous Vehicles:

Autonomous vehicles, also known as self-driving cars, are one of the most prominent applications of AI in transportation. These vehicles use AI algorithms, sensor systems, and advanced computer vision techniques to perceive and navigate the environment, making decisions and driving without human intervention.

Real-Life Example: Waymo, a subsidiary of Alphabet Inc. (Google), has been at the forefront of autonomous vehicle development.

Waymo's self-driving cars have driven millions of miles on public roads, demonstrating the potential of AI in transforming the future of transportation.

2. Traffic Management:

AI-powered traffic management systems analyse real-time data from various sources, such as traffic cameras, sensors, and GPS devices, to optimize traffic flow, reduce congestion, and improve overall transportation efficiency. These systems can dynamically adjust traffic signal timings, predict traffic patterns, and suggest alternative routes to alleviate congestion.

Real-Life Example: Singapore's Intelligent Transport System uses AI algorithms to manage traffic congestion in real time. The system collects data from various sources and adjusts traffic signal timings, accordingly, resulting in smoother traffic flow and reduced travel times.

3. Predictive Maintenance:

AI algorithms can analyse sensor data and vehicle performance metrics to predict maintenance needs, detect anomalies, and identify potential failures in transportation systems. By proactively addressing maintenance issues, transportation providers can minimize downtime, improve safety, and optimize maintenance schedules.

Real-Life Example: German railway company Deutsche Bahn uses AI-based predictive maintenance systems to monitor its trains and railway infrastructure. By analysing sensor data, the system can detect potential faults and schedule maintenance activities before major breakdowns occur, ensuring safe and reliable train operations.

4. Intelligent Transportation Systems (ITS):

AI is driving the development of intelligent transportation systems, which integrate various technologies, including AI, to improve safety, efficiency, and sustainability in transportation. These systems encompass features such as real-time traffic monitoring, incident detection, dynamic route guidance, and integration with other modes of transportation.

Real-Life Example: The City of Los Angeles implemented an AI-powered traffic management system called LA Optimized Traffic Signals (LAOTS). The system uses AI algorithms to dynamically adjust traffic signal timings based on real-time traffic conditions, reducing congestion, and improving traffic flow.

Conclusion:

The integration of AI in transportation, particularly in autonomous vehicles and intelligent transportation systems, is transforming the way we move and commute. Real-life examples, such as Waymo's autonomous vehicles, Singapore's Intelligent Transport System, Deutsche Bahn's predictive maintenance, and LA's AI-powered traffic management system, highlight the tangible benefits of AI in improving transportation safety, efficiency, and sustainability.

However, the widespread adoption of AI in transportation faces challenges such as regulatory frameworks, safety concerns, and public acceptance. Addressing these challenges requires collaboration between technology companies, transportation providers, policymakers, and society at large to ensure a responsible and seamless transition to AI-powered transportation systems.

As AI continues to advance, applications in transportation are expected to expand further, enabling the development of smart cities, efficient mobility solutions, and enhanced safety on roads. By harnessing the power of AI, the transportation industry can create a future where transportation is safer, more efficient, and accessible for all.

PART IV: FUTURE DIRECTIONS AND CHALLENGES

CHAPTER 19: CURRENT TRENDS AND STATE-OF-THE-ART IN AI AND GPT

Introduction:

Artificial Intelligence (AI) and Generative Pre-trained Transformers (GPT) have witnessed significant advancements in recent years, transforming various industries and pushing the boundaries of what machines can achieve. In this chapter, we will explore the current trends and state-of-the-art in AI and GPT, discussing the latest developments, applications, and the impact they have on society. Real-life examples will be provided to illustrate the cutting-edge advancements in these fields.

1. Deep Learning and Neural Networks:

Deep learning, a subset of AI, has emerged as a powerful tool for solving complex problems by mimicking the human brain's neural networks. State-of-the-art deep learning models, such as convolutional neural networks (CNNs) and recurrent neural networks (RNNs), have achieved remarkable results in computer vision, natural language processing, and speech recognition.

Real-Life Example: Image recognition systems powered by deep learning, such as Google's Inception and Facebook's DeepFace, have surpassed human performance in tasks like object recognition and facial recognition, enabling applications like image-based search and biometric authentication.

2. Reinforcement Learning and AI Agents:

Reinforcement learning is an area of AI that focuses on training agents to make sequential decisions based on rewards and punishments. State-of-the-art algorithms, such as deep Q-networks (DQNs) and Proximal Policy Optimization (PPO), have achieved impressive results in game-playing, robotics, and control systems.

Real-Life Example: AlphaGo, developed by DeepMind, a subsidiary of Alphabet Inc., became the first AI program to defeat a human world champion in the ancient board game Go. AlphaGo's success demonstrated the potential of reinforcement learning in mastering complex strategic games.

3. Natural Language Processing (NLP) Advancements:

NLP, a branch of AI focused on understanding and processing human language, has witnessed significant advancements with the rise of GPT models. State-of-the-art language models, such as GPT-3, have demonstrated impressive language generation, comprehension, and translation capabilities.

Real-Life Example: OpenAI's GPT-3 has been used to develop chatbots, language translation systems, and content generation tools. Its ability to generate human-like text has raised both excitement and concerns about the potential impact on content creation and misinformation.

4. Explainable AI (XAI):

As AI models become more complex, there is a growing need for explain ability, ensuring that AI systems can provide interpretable explanations for their decisions. State-of-the-art techniques, such as attention mechanisms and model-agnostic interpretability methods, are being developed to enhance the transparency and trustworthiness of AI systems.

Real-Life Example: IBM's AI Explain ability 360 toolkit provides developers with tools and algorithms to interpret and explain the decisions made by AI models. This helps ensure accountability and enables users to understand why a particular decision was made.

Conclusion:

The current trends and state-of-the-art in AI and GPT are continually evolving, pushing the boundaries of what machines can achieve. Deep learning, reinforcement learning, NLP advancements, and explainable AI are some of the key areas driving innovation in the field. Real-life examples like Google's Inception, DeepMind's AlphaGo, OpenAI's GPT-3, and IBM's AI Explain ability 360 toolkit demonstrate the transformative impact of these advancements.

As AI and GPT continue to progress, it is crucial to address ethical considerations, such as data privacy, algorithmic bias, and the potential displacement of jobs. Ongoing research and collaboration between academia, industry, and policymakers are essential to ensure the responsible development and deployment of AI technologies.

Looking ahead, the future of AI and GPT holds tremendous potential, with applications in healthcare, finance, manufacturing, and beyond. Continued advancements in these fields will shape the way we live, work, and interact with intelligent machines, leading to a future where AI and humans collaborate to solve complex problems and drive innovation.

CHAPTER 20: THE IMPACT OF AI ON THE JOB MARKET

Introduction:

Artificial Intelligence (AI) is revolutionizing industries and transforming the way we work. As AI technologies continue to advance, there is growing concern about their impact on the job market. In this chapter, we will explore the various ways AI is influencing employment, discussing the potential benefits and challenges it presents. Real-life examples will be provided to illustrate the impact of AI on different sectors of the job market.

1. Automation and Job Displacement:

One of the primary concerns regarding AI is the potential for automation to replace human workers. AI-powered systems and robots can perform routine and repetitive tasks more efficiently and accurately, leading to job displacement in certain industries.

Real-Life Example: In the manufacturing sector, the introduction of AI-powered robots has led to the automation of assembly lines and production processes, reducing the need for manual labour. Companies like Tesla and Amazon have implemented robotic systems to improve efficiency and productivity in their operations.

2. Augmentation of Human Capabilities:

While AI has the potential to automate certain tasks, it can also enhance human capabilities and create new job opportunities. AI technologies can assist humans in performing complex tasks, making them more productive and efficient.

Real-Life Example: In the healthcare industry, AI-powered systems can analyse medical data and assist doctors in diagnosing diseases. IBM's Watson, for instance, has been used to analyse medical images and provide insights to healthcare professionals, improving accuracy and efficiency in diagnosis.

3. Emergence of New Job Roles:

As AI technologies continue to evolve, new job roles and skill sets are emerging. There is a growing demand for AI specialists, data scientists, machine learning engineers, and other professionals with expertise in AI-related fields.

Real-Life Example: Companies like Google, Microsoft, and Amazon are actively recruiting AI specialists and investing in AI research and development. The demand for professionals with AI skills is expected to grow exponentially in the coming years.

4. Reskilling and Upskilling:

To adapt to the changing job landscape, individuals and organizations need to invest in reskilling and upskilling programs. By acquiring new skills and knowledge related to AI and its applications, individuals can remain competitive in the job market.

Real-Life Example: Companies like AT&T and IBM have implemented programs to reskill their workforce in AI-related technologies. They provide training and resources to help employees transition into new roles that align with the evolving needs of the industry.

5. Ethical Considerations and Social Impacts:

AI's impact on the job market raises ethical considerations and social implications. It is crucial to address concerns such as algorithmic bias, privacy, and the potential for job polarization to ensure that AI technologies are deployed responsibly.

Real-Life Example: The use of AI algorithms in recruitment processes has raised concerns about bias and discrimination. In 2018, Amazon discontinued an AI-powered recruiting tool after it was found to be biased against female applicants.

Conclusion:

AI is reshaping the job market, bringing both opportunities and challenges. While some jobs may be at risk of automation, AI also presents new possibilities and the need for skilled professionals in AI-related fields. Reskilling and upskilling programs, along with responsible deployment of AI technologies, are essential to navigate the evolving job landscape.

To mitigate the potential negative impact on employment, policymakers, businesses, and educational institutions must collaborate to ensure a smooth transition and provide support for individuals affected by AI-driven changes. By embracing the transformative power of AI and fostering a culture of lifelong learning, we can adapt to the evolving job market and unlock the full potential of AI to drive innovation and economic growth.

CHAPTER 21: ENSURING FAIRNESS AND BIAS

Mitigation in AI

Introduction:

Artificial Intelligence (AI) systems have the potential to shape and influence various aspects of our lives, from decision-making processes to resource allocation. However, there is a growing concern about the fairness and potential biases embedded in AI algorithms. In this chapter, we will explore the importance of ensuring fairness and discuss strategies to mitigate bias in AI systems. Real-life examples will be provided to illustrate the challenges and progress in this area.

1. Understanding Bias in AI:

AI algorithms learn from vast amounts of data, which can inadvertently encode biases present in the data. Biases can emerge due to various factors, such as historical inequalities, unrepresentative data samples, or biased human judgments. It is essential to identify and address these biases to ensure fair and unbiased outcomes.

Real-Life Example: In 2018, Google's image recognition algorithm was found to misclassify images of people of colour more frequently than those of white individuals. This highlighted the presence of racial bias in the training data and underscored the need for bias mitigation strategies.

2. Fairness Metrics and Measures:

To address bias in AI systems, researchers and practitioners have developed fairness metrics and measures. These metrics quantify the fairness of an algorithm's outcomes across different demographic groups. By analysing these metrics, biases can be identified, and appropriate measures can be taken to mitigate them.

Real-Life Example: ProPublica, a non-profit news organization, investigated the COMPAS algorithm used in the criminal justice system to predict the likelihood of reoffending. They found that the algorithm was biased against black defendants, leading to higher false positive rates. This case sparked discussions about fairness and the need to re-evaluate the use of AI in the criminal justice system.

3. Bias Mitigation Techniques:

Several techniques have been developed to mitigate bias in AI systems. These include pre-processing the data to remove bias, re-weighting the data to ensure equal representation, and adjusting the algorithm's decision-making process to account for fairness considerations. Regular monitoring and evaluation of AI systems are crucial to identify and address biases that may arise during their operation.

Real-Life Example: Facebook implemented a tool called Fairness Flow to measure and mitigate biases in its algorithms. The tool helps identify potential biases in content ranking, advertising, and other AI-driven processes, allowing for corrective actions to be taken to ensure fairness.

4. Diverse and Inclusive Data Collection:

To mitigate bias, it is essential to ensure that the data used to train AI algorithms is diverse, inclusive, and representative of the populations affected by the algorithms' decisions. This requires careful consideration of data collection processes and taking steps to address underrepresentation and biases in the data.

Real-Life Example: The ImageNet dataset, a widely used dataset for training image recognition algorithms, was found to have biased labels, including offensive or stereotypical terms. Efforts are being made to create more inclusive datasets that accurately represent the diversity of the real world.

5. Ethical Considerations and Transparency:

Addressing bias in AI systems goes beyond technical measures. It requires ethical considerations and transparency in the development, deployment, and use of AI technologies. Ethical frameworks and guidelines can guide ensuring fairness, accountability, and transparency in AI systems.

Real-Life Example: The European Union's General Data Protection Regulation (GDPR) includes provisions that emphasize the need for explain ability and transparency in automated decision-making processes, including those driven by AI.

Conclusion:

Ensuring fairness and mitigating bias in AI systems is crucial to prevent discrimination, promote equal opportunities, and build trust in AI technologies. Efforts are being made by researchers, policymakers, and organizations to develop tools, techniques, and guidelines to address bias and promote fairness in AI systems. However, challenges remain, and the pursuit of fairness in AI requires ongoing research, collaboration, and a commitment to ethical principles. By addressing bias and striving for fairness, we can harness the full potential of AI to benefit all individuals and create a more equitable society.

CHAPTER 22: AI SAFETY AND ROBUSTNESS

Introduction:

As artificial intelligence (AI) systems become increasingly powerful and pervasive, ensuring their safety and robustness becomes paramount. In this chapter, we will explore the importance of AI safety and discuss strategies to enhance the reliability and resilience of AI systems. Real-life examples will be provided to illustrate the challenges and progress in this area.

1. The Need for AI Safety:

AI systems have the potential to make critical decisions that impact human lives and societal well-being. Therefore, it is crucial to develop AI systems that are safe, trustworthy, and resilient. AI safety focuses on mitigating risks associated with unintended consequences, system failures, and malicious use of AI technology.

Real-Life Example: In 2016, Microsoft launched a Twitter chatbot named Tay. Within hours of its release, the chatbot started posting offensive and inappropriate tweets, reflecting the dangers of AI systems being manipulated by malicious actors. This incident highlighted the importance of ensuring AI safety.

2. Robustness in AI Systems:

Robustness refers to the ability of an AI system to perform well under various conditions and against different types of threats or attacks. Robust AI systems are less susceptible to adversarial manipulation, data perturbations, or algorithmic biases. Achieving robustness involves techniques such as adversarial training, input sanitization, and model regularization.

Real-Life Example: DeepMind, a leading AI research organization, developed an adversarial training technique called "Adversarial Reprogramming" to make AI systems more robust against adversarial attacks. This technique involves training the AI system to resist manipulation and maintain its intended behaviour even when faced with malicious input.

3. Verification and Validation of AI Systems:

Verification and validation methods play a crucial role in ensuring the safety and reliability of AI systems. These methods involve rigorous testing, verification of system properties and validation against predefined specifications. Formal methods, such as formal verification and model checking, can provide mathematical guarantees about the behaviour and safety of AI systems.

Real-Life Example: NASA extensively uses verification and validation techniques to ensure the safety of AI systems in spacecraft operations. These techniques help verify that the AI algorithms meet the desired specifications and perform as intended in critical space missions.

4. Ethical Considerations and Human Oversight:

AI safety also encompasses ethical considerations and human oversight in the development and deployment of AI systems. Ethical frameworks and guidelines help address concerns related to fairness, privacy, accountability, and transparency. Human oversight ensures that AI systems are used responsibly, and that human values and ethical principles are respected.

Real-Life Example: The autonomous vehicle industry incorporates safety measures that prioritize human well-being. For example, self-driving cars are programmed to prioritize pedestrian safety and follow traffic laws, highlighting the importance of ethical considerations and human oversight in AI systems.

5. Continual Learning and Adaptation:

AI safety requires the ability to continually learn and adapt to new circumstances and challenges. Ongoing monitoring, feedback loops, and system updates are necessary to address emerging risks and vulnerabilities. Regular audits, testing, and retraining of AI systems can ensure their performance remains robust and aligned with desired outcomes.

Real-Life Example: OpenAI, an AI research organization, implemented a process called "AI Safety via Debate" to train AI models to reason and argue ethically. This approach involves iterative training and refinement to improve the safety and reliability of AI systems.

Conclusion:

AI safety and robustness are vital for the responsible development and deployment of AI technologies. As AI becomes increasingly integrated into various domains, ensuring the safety and reliability of AI systems becomes paramount. By addressing challenges related to AI safety, enhancing robustness, and considering ethical considerations, we can maximize the benefits of AI while minimizing the risks. The development of standards, guidelines, and regulatory frameworks is crucial to ensure the safe and trustworthy use of AI systems. Continued research, collaboration, and public engagement are essential to advance AI safety and build a future where AI technologies contribute to human well-being and societal progress.

CHAPTER 23: THE FUTURE OF AI AND GPT: PREDICTIONS AND SPECULATIONS

Introduction:
The field of artificial intelligence (AI) and the development of advanced language models, such as Generative Pre-trained Transformers (GPT), have witnessed rapid progress in recent years. As we look ahead, it is intriguing to explore the potential future advancements and speculate on the possibilities that lie ahead. In this chapter, we will discuss predictions and speculations about the future of AI and GPT, considering their impact on various domains and the challenges they may pose.

1. Continued Advancements in AI Technology:
AI technology is expected to continue evolving and improving in the coming years. With advancements in deep learning, reinforcement learning, and neural networks, AI systems will become more sophisticated, capable of complex tasks, and better at understanding and interacting with humans.

Real-Life Example: OpenAI's GPT-3, released in 2020, demonstrated significant advancements in natural language understanding and generation. The model showcased the potential for AI to generate coherent and contextually relevant text, paving the way for future developments in language processing and communication.

2. Enhanced Human-AI Collaboration:

As AI technology progresses, the focus will shift towards enhancing human-AI collaboration. AI systems will serve as intelligent assistants, augmenting human capabilities and supporting decision-making processes. The synergy between humans and AI will enable more efficient problem-solving, creative endeavours, and innovation.

Real-Life Example: The use of AI-powered virtual assistants like Siri, Google Assistant, and Alexa has become increasingly common. These assistants provide personalized recommendations, assist in performing tasks, and improve user experiences, highlighting the potential of human-AI collaboration.

3. Ethical and Responsible AI Development:

As AI becomes more pervasive, the ethical and responsible development and use of AI systems will become a critical consideration. Efforts will be made to address concerns related to bias, privacy, transparency, and accountability. Ethical frameworks and regulations will be established to ensure that AI technologies are developed and deployed in a manner that aligns with societal values and respects human rights.

Real-Life Example: The European Union's General Data Protection Regulation (GDPR) sets guidelines for the ethical and responsible use of AI systems. It emphasizes the importance of transparency, data protection, and accountability in AI development and deployment.

4. AI in Healthcare and Medicine:

AI will play a significant role in revolutionizing healthcare and medicine. AI-powered diagnostic systems, personalized medicine, drug discovery, and patient monitoring will become more prevalent. AI algorithms will analyse vast amounts of medical data, leading to faster and more accurate diagnoses and treatment recommendations.

Real-Life Example: IBM's Watson for Oncology is an AI system that assists healthcare professionals in making treatment decisions for cancer patients. By analysing medical literature, patient records, and clinical guidelines, Watson provides evidence-based treatment options, empowering physicians with valuable insights.

5. AI in Sustainability and Climate Change:
AI technology will be harnessed to address environmental challenges and promote sustainability. AI-powered systems can optimize energy consumption, improve resource management, and aid in climate modelling and prediction. The integration of AI with renewable energy sources and smart grids will contribute to a more sustainable future.

Real-Life Example: Google's DeepMind developed an AI system that optimizes the cooling systems in data centres, reducing energy consumption by up to 40%. This example demonstrates the potential of AI to drive sustainability efforts.

Conclusion:
The future of AI and GPT holds tremendous promise and potential. With continued advancements, AI technology will transform various industries, augment human capabilities, and address societal challenges. Ethical considerations, responsible development, and human-AI collaboration will be crucial in shaping the future landscape of AI. As we move forward, it is essential to foster a multidisciplinary approach, engage in public discourse, and establish policies and guidelines to ensure the responsible and beneficial use of AI. By embracing the possibilities of AI and addressing its challenges, we can harness its power to create a future that benefits all of humanity.

CHAPTER 24: ETHICAL CONSIDERATIONS AND RESPONSIBLE AI DEVELOPMENT

Introduction:
As artificial intelligence (AI) continues to advance and become more integrated into various aspects of our lives, it is essential to address the ethical considerations and ensure responsible development and deployment of AI systems. In this chapter, we will explore the key ethical considerations associated with AI and discuss the principles and frameworks that guide responsible AI development.

1. Transparency and Explain ability:
Transparency in AI systems is crucial to building trust and understanding among users and stakeholders. It involves providing clear explanations of how AI systems make decisions, what data they use, and the potential biases or limitations they may have. Explain ability enables users to comprehend the reasoning behind AI-generated outcomes and facilitates the identification of potential errors or biases.

Real-Life Example: The European Union's General Data Protection Regulation (GDPR) includes a "right to explanation" that provides individuals with the right to know the logic behind automated decisions that affect them. This emphasizes the importance of transparency in AI systems.

2. Fairness and Bias Mitigation:
Ensuring fairness in AI systems is vital to prevent discriminatory outcomes and biases. Developers must strive to eliminate biases in training data and algorithms to avoid perpetuating unfair practices or marginalizing certain individuals or groups. Techniques like data augmentation, bias detection, and algorithmic fairness can help mitigate biases and promote equitable outcomes.

Real-Life Example: In 2015, Amazon developed an AI-powered recruiting tool that showed a bias against female candidates. The system was trained on historical resumes, which were predominantly from male applicants, leading to biased recommendations. This example highlights the importance of addressing biases in AI systems to ensure fairness.

3. Privacy and Data Protection:
Responsible AI development requires safeguarding user privacy and protecting sensitive data. Developers must adhere to legal and ethical guidelines for data collection, storage, and usage. Privacy-preserving techniques such as differential privacy and federated learning can be employed to minimize data exposure while still enabling effective AI algorithms.

Real-Life Example: Apple's Face ID technology utilizes on-device processing and encryption to protect user biometric data, ensuring that sensitive facial recognition information remains secure and private.

4. Accountability and Governance:
Establishing accountability mechanisms and governance frameworks is crucial to ensure that AI systems are developed and used responsibly. This includes identifying clear lines of responsibility for AI decision-making, establishing oversight mechanisms, and implementing processes for addressing issues

or unintended consequences.

Real-Life Example: The Partnership on AI is a collaborative initiative that brings together leading organizations to develop and promote best practices in AI. It aims to foster accountability and transparency in AI development and deployment.

5. Social Impact and Inclusivity:
Consideration of the social impact of AI is essential to avoid exacerbating existing societal inequalities. Developers should strive to create AI systems that benefit a diverse range of users and address the needs of marginalized communities. Inclusive design practices, diverse and representative datasets, and user feedback mechanisms can help ensure that AI benefits all members of society.

Real-Life Example: Google's Project Euphonia aims to improve automatic speech recognition for individuals with speech impairments. By including diverse voices and addressing specific needs, this project demonstrates the potential of AI to promote inclusivity.

Conclusion:
Ethical considerations and responsible AI development are critical in shaping the future of AI. Transparency, fairness, privacy, accountability, and inclusivity should guide the development and deployment of AI systems. Real-life examples highlight the need for ethical practices and responsible AI development to prevent biases, protect privacy, and ensure equitable outcomes. By adopting ethical frameworks, fostering collaboration, and incorporating diverse perspectives, we can harness the power of AI to create a more inclusive and beneficial future for all.

Conclusion:
Recapitulation and Final Thoughts on the Future of AI and GPT

In this concluding chapter, we will recapitulate the key points discussed throughout the book and provide final thoughts on the future of artificial intelligence (AI) and Generative Pre-trained Transformers (GPT). We have explored the evolution of AI, the concepts and terminology associated with it, and the transformative impact of GPT in various fields. Now, let us reflect on the significance of these advancements and contemplate the path ahead.

Recapitulation:
Throughout this book, we have delved into the history of AI, from its early beginnings to its current state-of-the-art technologies. We explored the different machine learning algorithms and techniques that power AI systems and the deep learning architectures that enable complex pattern recognition. We discussed the application of AI in natural language processing, image and video processing, healthcare, finance, manufacturing, and transportation. We also explored the ethical considerations and responsible development of AI, including fairness, privacy, accountability, and inclusivity.

Final Thoughts:

1. Accelerating Innovation: The rapid progress in AI, fuelled by breakthroughs in deep learning and neural networks, has opened new possibilities and opportunities across industries. As technology continues to advance, we can expect AI to play an increasingly significant role in solving complex problems, driving innovation, and transforming various aspects of our lives.

2. Ethical Considerations: As AI becomes more prevalent, it is crucial to address the ethical implications associated with its development and deployment. We must prioritize fairness, transparency, and accountability to ensure that AI systems are designed and used responsibly, avoiding biases and discrimination.

3. Collaboration and Regulation: The future of AI requires collaboration among stakeholders, including researchers,

developers, policymakers, and ethicists. By working together, we can establish regulatory frameworks, industry standards, and best practices that promote the responsible and beneficial use of AI.

4. Continuous Learning: AI is an ever-evolving field, and it is essential for professionals to engage in continuous learning and stay updated with the latest advancements. As AI technologies progress, it is crucial to adapt and develop the necessary skills to harness the potential of AI and contribute to its responsible development and application.

5. Societal Impact: AI has the potential to address societal challenges, improve efficiency, and enhance human lives. However, it is important to ensure that AI technologies are developed with a human-centric approach, considering their impact on individuals, communities, and society.

Real-Life Examples:

- Self-driving cars: Companies like Tesla and Waymo are developing autonomous vehicles powered by AI. These vehicles have the potential to enhance road safety, reduce traffic congestion, and improve transportation efficiency.

- Personalized healthcare: AI algorithms can analyse large volumes of medical data to identify patterns, make accurate diagnoses, and personalize treatment plans. This can lead to improved patient outcomes and more efficient healthcare delivery.

- Virtual assistants: Voice-activated virtual assistants like Amazon's Alexa and Apple's Siri utilize AI technologies to understand and respond to user commands. These assistants have become integral parts of many households, providing convenience and assistance in various tasks.

Conclusion:
Artificial intelligence and GPT have revolutionized the way we

interact with technology and have the potential to shape our future in profound ways. As we move forward, it is crucial to balance innovation with ethical considerations, ensuring that AI is developed and deployed responsibly. By fostering collaboration, embracing continuous learning, and considering the societal impact, we can harness the power of AI to address complex challenges and create a better future for all. The journey of AI and GPT is ongoing, and it is up to us to shape it with wisdom, responsibility, and a commitment to the well-being of humanity.

www.ingramcontent.com/pod-product-compliance
Lightning Source LLC
LaVergne TN
LVHW051537050326
832903LV00033B/4286